Lacuna

Kieran Davis

Best wishes

Kieran Davis

Lacuna

Kieran Davis

Edited by Black Pear Press

First published in July 2016 by Black Pear Press
www.blackpear.net

ISBN 978-1-910322-24-6

Cover Photograph and Design by Damien Davis
http://damiendavis.co.uk

Black Pear Press

Introduction

People who read poems love language. People who read poetry love life. They devour it, ever hungry for the next experience. Most people leave a poem's page with a sense of empathy, sometimes even a knowing smile. And if they encountered poetry whilst they were there, they will have discovered, with great relief, they are not alone.

Lacuna's message is simple: no secret is forever but don't search too hard for the parts that are missing, sometimes, they're not meant to be found.

lacuna *n., pl.* **—nae** (-nee) or **—nas.** 1. An empty space or missing part, especially in an ancient manuscript; a gap. 2. *Biology.* A cavity or depression.

Dedication

This should have been the short and simple page that acknowledged someone for their influence. The dedication was an obvious choice but not one taken lightly. I overthought the notion. I considered dedicating the book to poetry, but that felt pretentious. I dreamed of dedicating *Lacuna* to an invented character, a pointless puzzle to confuse and infuriate, accentuating the title. I nurtured the idea of dedicating the piece to all those who believed in me, supported me, but that would have taken pages (I am a most fortunate man and grateful to you all). I even thought of dedicating it to dedication, for it has been twenty (ish) years of doing so that has led to a publication of my own. Heck, in order not to disappoint anyone who thought they deserved the dedication, I surmised dedicating *Lacuna* to biscuits (I love biscuits). And whilst there are several acknowledgements to be found, there is only one person that could ever furnish this page with their name. This book is lovingly dedicated to my beautiful wife.

For Siân

Immortal beloved, I am because you are.

Because of you: non omnis moriar.

vi

Contents

Every Stone A Memory

Every stone, a memory;
every leaf, a dream;
every stick, a story
sailing on a stream.
Every acorn, a reminder;
every breeze, a theme;
every song will bind her,
turn a whisper to a scream.

Sea-side Reverie

I see the waves,
can hear the sea,
it whispers in my memory.
I feel the sand,
soft underfoot,
the sense of something
that I put
away, and ready
for a rhyme,
a poem of another time,
when the salty smell
that, of course, could
invade a thought
of childhood,
when I saw the waves
and heard the sea
that whispers in my memory.

Finders Keepers

I am not permitted to give you presents,
it is against the rules
—but if I were to leave this—
by accident, it would appear.
Perhaps you would find it,
pick it up by complete chance
and treasure it;
remembering a young man
with old eyes
and a laughing heart.

Working Class Faith And Politics

Did we rise above the peasantry
in our quest to become better?
Ignorance fed arrogance,
the yokes none could unfetter,
proud of our work ethics,
but burning to be more
than we earned, how we yearned,
for fortune's fatal flaw.

We played at being yuppies,
in our shirts and shiny shoes,
rented righteous resolutions,
believed we'd paid our dues,
and we whored away the destiny,
that we once thought we deserved,
so we could cheat the ferryman,
our legacy preserved.

Fragment

Arms tucked under our knees,
we sit at the top of the fire escape,
heads together in reverie.
You gaze over the play-park, lost,
whilst I think how the banister needs
some varnish or perhaps a coat of paint.

Nothing to say that makes sense,
I taste your tears in a kiss,
worrying over your beautiful eyes
that destroy me with their sadness,
I know you will write, you know I will call,
but it's so far away, so very far away.

And you wrap yourself around me,
envelop me in all I ever wanted,
all that I am going to lose;
I hear no music, cry no tears;
it does not feel real.
I will wait for the rain and...Oh.

A Hundred Pages

The sand beneath my toes,
as I wander distant shores,
reminds me of reality,
old aches, imagined sores,
the scars of half a life-time,
across a hundred pages,
collected works considered
by lovers, fools and sages.

Murder Most Magnificent

for Paul F. Lenzi

The cell walls felt colder,
the sense of imprisonment,
more profound and terrifying,
as murder upon murder
of crows lay siege to the tower,
a cacophony of chaos,
aching in my nightmare.

Candle Haiku

The tide ebbing flow
spirit burns with moonlight glow
candle burning low

Gladiatorial Calligraphy

The graffiti painted on my soul,
tattoo tags of poetry and prostitution,
an artful mess to less discerning eyes,
my ink-stained heart, an arena
for fallen faiths and their institution.

Believed To Be Misconceived

or 'Misquoted'

Taste my hate and hunger,
waste my blaze, be free,
chase my will and wonder,
take my ashes out to sea.

Searching For Silence

Silence is golden,
or so they say,
I think of it more
like silver,
a more delicate and
subtle beauty
that makes me smile
at the luxury,
a most priceless
commodity that costs
no more than the desire
to seek it,
the quintessential quietude.
Searching for silence:
A quest for a noble heart.

Lovely Lies

or 'Shame'

"Hello, sweetie-pie,
just letting you know,
my train is arriving
and I'll be home soon.
I love you too."
Delight in her eyes,
an authenticity,
a declaration
forced, it fades quickly,
mouth turned down,
smile disappearing,
to be expeditiously replaced
by sudden sadness.
Her pretty face,
poisoned by a frown,
such sorrow evident,
eyes glisten
with emotion
and so the ruse, the lie,
the "I love you too."
I wondered,
when would she tell him?
A sorry state,
keeping sadness a secret,
dirty, dirty shame.
Shame…

Oh, Sleep!

Oh, sleep, my enemy!
I long to wrest control,
rid myself of you entirely,
this tiredness in my soul.
Light, give me sobriety!
A constant conscious thought,
I yearn to accomplish,
let the day not be for naught.

Sleep, my estranged friend,
wherever did you go?
I cannot rest (and must attest)
I truly miss you so.
The night seems eternal,
the day gone in a blink,
I cannot stop thinking,
nor can I sleep a wink.

The Circle

for the Worcester Writers' Circle

It stands for integrity,
creativity and fun,
talented individuals,
come together as one,
a coven of careful activity,
companions, second-to-none,
poets, playwrights, storytellers,
you can't have a circle of one.

Dance Of The Butterfly

I watched white wings of gossamer,
enchant a breeze, a lost glamour,
a cantrip cast, that had escaped
the wizened wizard who just gaped
at the majesty of nature's spell,
the butterfly who will never tell
how simple it is to thwart, be strange
to magic on the winds of change.

A Cure For The Disease

Weathered words of warning,
ignored by the impatient,
fervid fools who fake art,
accept that which they did not
earn or deserve, with smiles
that do not meet the eyes, the lies,
of children armed to the teeth
and unable to appreciate life
for what it is, their potential,
stifled by their choice of entertainment:
The misery of others which they
use to smother the love
they never received from their mothers.

The Lesser Pebbles

She picked up a pebble and threw it,
with a twist of her slender wrist,
making it skim the silver lake,
the stone bounced off the glassy surface,
leaving a trail of ripples that faded
into nothing, leaving no evidence
that it had ever existed before centuries,
of lying dormant on the water's bed,
awaiting erosion.
Still—the stone had at least had
the chance to dance—
during its time on earth.
What of the lesser pebbles?

Discovery Beyond Recovery

The poem poured out
onto tired looking paper,
where bored individuals
took turns to rape her,
dissecting, infecting,
disgusting theory,
whilst words withered, wondering,
why do they fear me?
Imaginations stifled,
they rifled through text books,
terrible teaching,
received only vexed looks,
schooled in deciphering,
kept under heel,
the poem wept
for they did not feel.

The Hug

I held on to the night, to the theory
that this recollection of your heart,
thumping the same rhythm as mine was
a true sentiment, not a settlement.
I held tight to the promontory,
the edge of reason, that precarious step
to the precipice of emoting without fear
of humiliation. I hugged all this in the
hope of holding more than a memory.

Note from the poet: I read a wonderful poem by a lady called
Tess Gallagher, also called 'The Hug' that really sat well with
me and I'd like to quote a few lines from stanza five:

'Clearly, a little permission
Is a dangerous thing.
But when you hug someone
You want it to be a masterpiece
Of connection.'

I am still contemplating the first line, which felt profound and
deserving of attention, that thought on wanting the hug to be
a masterpiece was superb. It is something I am certain we all
believe to be true (I know I want all my hugs to be
remembered!). There was something deeper here for me
though, I felt that I wanted to give more, that a hug doesn't
necessarily have to be made of physical contact. Some poets
have the ability to hold me intimately with a line, lovingly with
a verse or reassuringly with an idea. Others hug me as a
welcome companion, that awkward manly pat on the back or
tender womanly squeeze that says 'there is something about
you that I cherish' and all they need do to accomplish this is
write a poem. Hug someone today, I dare you.

Deciduous

or 'Falling Leaves'

I watch the wind-blown leaves
in a flurry of colourful play,
thinking the scattered leavings
seem in a hurry as they sway.
Dust and debris settle
in a destined pattern on the path,
I think not of home and hearth,
for I like this weather, laugh,
at raindrops drizzling an epitaph
against the glass, a smear, a stain,
of Autumn mulch from yesteryear,
sod-soaked memory lane.

The Farewell Spell

Laughter,
that was the sound that floated on the breeze:
laughter.
A lilting titter, melodious, infectious,
others in the congregation smiled and giggled.
Many wiped tears from their faces, unashamed
at their presence, as the laughter filled
the room and fled towards the cemetery.
The laughter tickled the trees, brushing
the grass and flowers with sunshine
before fading slowly like a memory.
And it did not seem inappropriate,
it was necessary, we believed.
He would have loved that there was laughter at his grave.

Sure Is Quiet

Listen,
wait,
listen,
realise,
no one listens.
Wait,
no one waits
for long
unless they listened.

Kiss Off, Cancer!

I wish I could kiss your
cancer goodbye,
hold you and tell you
there's no need to cry,
I wish I could kiss your,
cancer goodbye.

Abandoned

Where were you when I needed you?
   Helping you to hope.
And when I cried? When my faith died?
   Teaching you to cope.

Silhouette

Darkness, dancing on the walls,
a puppet of the light, an illusion
painted by the candles,
they were artists, whose pallet
had become an absence of form,
their brush, being
the very air we breathe,
a susurrus, splashing
shadows on to an obscure canvas,
the walls coming ever closer
in the mind's eye.
And the poet—
whose soul's valley becomes populated
with ghosts, memory and fervency—
writes poems for prisoners,
who know those walls all too well,
and the prisoners—whose crimes
are irrelevant when delivering love—
appreciate that colossal heart
and the wordsmith's dancing
silhouette.

Different

I like a variety
of textures and flavours,
a myriad of colour,
a mixture of behaviours,
I love to hear of different cultures,
hear other people's view,
make a magical memory,
experience something new.
I like to listen to music,
imagine the notes being chased,
melody, requiem, rhapsody,
I have quite eclectic taste.
I like to sample a spectrum
be different,
eat soup with a knife,
how I adore a 'mixed bag',
this buffet we call 'life'.

Thinker

Eyes glazed, I gazed at the shelf,
at enchiridions in the Thinkers' Library,
my fingers traced the cracked spines
of the dusty lines, no memory
recalling my feet falling towards
this bookcase, neglected by so many,
surprised to see here, Wells, H.G. —
in the same category of Sartre, J.P.

Theology, sociology, sex, faith, art,
metaphysics, mythology, all played a part
in creating philosophy and songs for *Singers*,
poetry, prose and ink-stained fingers,
the war of words, like Thor's thoughts of thunder,
the stench of the trench in a world torn asunder.

Smiling Assassin

Poke the bear,
tickle the troll,
tweak their cute little nose,
no visitor unwelcome
to poetry or prose,
take whatever you will
from passion and art,
read it, bleed it,
then depart
to court your fortune
with mistrust,
creativity, abused,
unjust, rust —
in peace, sweet
riddled rhapsody,
so obvious! You
rape my malady.

Elemental Me

I come to a place where I am lost,
a rare beauty to which I am blind,
up ahead, a quaquaversal signpost,
the curious crossroads in my mind,
I immure myself, lock up my emotions,
sell my soul for sand,
I could have made friends with my fortunes
but it was too heavy a price to land.

Too Late

I am pregnant.
I know, you whisper in my dreams.
I love you.
I heard you talking in your sleep.
I watch you.
I felt your eyes on me.
I feel you.
You touch me like you are my god.
I know you.
If only you could.
Hold me.
I have forgotten how.

Disguised By Joy

I wish I could read
what I'd written as a child,
when my English was poor,
imagination, wild,
when nothing was quiet,
the riot of play
would give me a story
in which I could stay,
under realms of wonder,
the thunder of joy,
when pencil and paper
became a loved toy.

Reason Tree

Relative reality,
rarely relieved,
unfairly relived,
barely believed.

Discovery

I looked out
and saw
nothing.
I gazed up
and knew
with perfect clarity,
I was…
insignificant
in comparison
to what was
possible.

Companion

Never alone
(well, hardly ever)
I feel more…clever
when on my own.

Estranged

Like a stranger in life's procession,
evidently able to lose one's self
in the world
more easily than end
the curses and misfortunes
that wed my obsessive,
compulsive, generosity.

Hilltop Encounter

or 'Subtle Seduction'

A hill-top encounter,
what might lie below?
The lights in the night
and the promise of snow.

Silence

The unsung melody
of all that is precious,
for only in that non-vocal
moment can there be clarity
and true consciousness.

The Christmas Day Killing

I walk across a murder scene
and utter not a word,
shoo away the dratted cat,
dispose of the bird,
I know it was only natural
for the animal to have toyed
but why in such a feral way?
I became annoyed
that life be taken on Christmas Day,
though I don't often think of Christ,
except at times such as this,
when Pagans sacrificed.
An offering of crimson blood
is like the circle closing,
gifts are given on this morn,
to abate forces opposing.

Cerulean Skies

Azure, so beautiful,
the green and grey of your eyes,
completing each other.
Love—like cerulean skies.

Colours painted by a god,
the green and grey of your eyes,
your majesty breathes promise.
Love—like cerulean skies.

Ink-Stained Fingers

I look at ink-stained fingers and smile,
not angry that the pen leaked,
as I realised in time, before it made a mess.
Others may easily have been enraged
by blue fingers that take days to return
to 'normal'.
I quite like it, feeling somewhat
comforted by the accident; the ink-stained
fingers make me feel like a scribe, a 'real'
writer for once, whatever a 'real' writer is,
I guess. I imagine a lovely wooden desk,
sturdy and durable, but attractive as much as
practical, maybe something in oak
like the pieces you see
on Antiques Road Show and look upon
with jealousy and desire,
intricate carving and a secret drawer.
I would cherish such a piece
of furniture and yearn to sit and write,
with ink-stained fingers and clean, crisp
parchment.
I could write a masterpiece with those,
I promise, with all of my heart.

Squeeze

Not sated, unsatisfied,
I burn with desire,
a soul seeped in sex,
trapped on a flaming pyre.
Love? Hah! Nonsense.
Her heart was a liar,
I yearn—damn—burn
and cannot escape the fire.

Soft and sinful, sensual,
you fuck all my flaws,
our mouths, desperate to taste,
our souls like gaping maws,
hungry for the touch,
desperate,
though beyond want, of course,
I need not to be in you but to *be* you,
I would be that close, all yours.

Because

I read because I can,
I write therefore I am,
I live, I love, I understand,
I read because I can,
I trust in the dust of the lore's demand,
I write therefore I am,
I read because I can,
I write therefore I am.

Couldn't Say

All is as it was,
as it has always been,
as it will always be,
for life's repetitive ways
can be kind and yet,
so very, very cruel,
tomorrow, but a memory,
of distant yesterdays.

Immortal Beloved

Sometimes I sit
in the silence
of my own soul,
serenading you
with a song
only your spirit
can hear,
an echo
of our wedding,
the miracle
of our marriage,
the family we forged;
the home in our hearts.
Whilst you breathe,
non omnis moriar.

Wordsmith

I wonder where the words go
when I'm not writing,
if I'm not even thinking
of letters.
To imagine syllables
in their own world,
a realm where they live free,
until another Wordsmith sets them
dancing on a page for me.

To think! Poems have lives of their own,
parts in a play, acts, yet unseen.
Memories and musings,
inklings so keen,
to leave their secret hideaway
and venture to the mind,
gifts so gratefully received,
and given back in kind.

I long for language to be liquid
so that I may imbibe
vast quantities like a drunkard,
an ever-thirsty scribe,
I fish for words in imagination,
with a blank page as my lure
and hope if poetry is a disease,
they never find a cure.

Absent Father

I worry about the world,
climate and finances,
I worry over your troubled heart
and long gone failed romances,
I worry that I will follow you
into madness and depression,
I worry what other people think,
my misconceived expression,
I worry about the ones I love
and wonder if they worry about me,
my worries can be consuming
and I worry constantly,
I worry about you being lonely,
I worry about you feeling blue,
I worry about your fear and panic,
I worry so much about you,
I worry that you worry,
I worry that you cannot cope,
but worry not because I love you
and I love to give you hope.

Dragonfly

A beautiful blue lady,
swimming in the sky,
from frond to frond, along the pond,
the dancing dragonfly.

The dizzy and yet dulcet sound
of her wings on high,
from frond to frond, along the pond,
the dancing dragonfly.

A butterfly died by the water's side,
but she had an alibi,
from frond to frond, along the pond,
the dancing dragonfly.

Naturally magic,
her beauty cannot die,
from frond to frond, along the pond,
the dancing dragonfly.

Proud, passionate, powerful,
she hunts hereby,
from frond to frond, along the pond,
the dancing dragonfly.

The paradise pool, like a screen,
a tool with which to scry,
from frond to frond, along the pond,
the dancing dragonfly.

Unbeliever overlook,
that which she personifies,
from frond to frond, along the pond,
the dancing dragonfly.

Her song, like a hymn,
a lilting lullaby,
from frond to frond, along the pond,
the dancing dragonfly.

If the will is to be enchanted,
she will edify,
from frond to frond, along the pond,
the dancing dragonfly.

A beautiful, blue lady,
swimming in the sky,
from frond to frond, along the pond,
the dancing dragonfly.

Corpse

The colour drained
from the sun, a feeling
of silent thunder,
as though dark deities
had devised emotions
out of emptiness.

Sadness, overwhelming
and complete
in its depressing entirety,
drifted like a gloomy mist
as the body
floated downstream.

Shadow In The Mirror

Sleeping with serpents,
sibilant sounds,
sing songs of sin and silence,
angers and astounds,
invokes imagined inadequacies,
whispers 'the craft of the wise',
loves lost languages,
such clever, clever lies.

Letter From Hell

We've made you a reservation,
kept your usual room,
we knew you could not stay away,
we sensed your doom and gloom,
so we've made you up a bed of nails,
for ultimate malaise,
we can't wait to see you lose
your temper with the blaze;
we hope you'll stay unhappy,
that your mind remains unwell,
you'll never outstay your welcome,
welcome back to hell.

Decided

I have made up my mind,
a ridiculous notion.
One may make a decision
but it is not possible
to make up a mind; that vessel
is always filling, forming
and formulating. Thoughts,
—whether consciously
continuing or not—occur
consistently, in a never-ending,
education of the self, beliefs
are conceived and truths
are believed, designed,
but one can never
make up a mind!

Auger

Shadows whisper their secrets to me,
the night, annotating a poem I feel,
as the river dictates to destiny,
how to make belief in illusion, real,
the torn tarot card tells me a story
and this sceptic must atone
for you stand before me.
I cease to be alone.

Hit 'n Run

I sat with the cat
while it died,
I sat with the cat
and I cried,
because I stopped
as the cat's clogs popped,
I lost something inside,
I sat with the cat
and I cried,
I sat with the cat
while it died.

Note from the poet: In my early teens, roaming the streets of
Gravesend, Kent, I saw an odd shape tucked up against a curb.
At first I thought it was a discarded black bin-bag but on
closer inspection, I realised it was a cat. The animal was
beautiful and I thought it was strange that it did not try to run
away like most cats when confronted with a stranger, so I knelt
down; I sensed something was wrong. It turned its head and
looked at me, small tongue hanging out of its mouth and
blood escaping its ears, breathing raggedly with an occasional
wheeze. One of its legs was bent the wrong way and it was
clear it had been hit or run over by a car. The driver hadn't
stopped to see if the cat was hurt (which may have saved its
life, who knows?). I stroked its head and sat on the curb,
praying its pain would end. I tentatively stroked its cheek as
the light left its eyes. It only took a few moments for the
animal to pass but it felt like an eternity. I knocked on the
nearest door and the occupant phoned a local vet to take care
of the body and inform the RSPCA. I didn't give a thought to
its owner, there was no name tag or contact number as the cat
wasn't wearing a collar.
I am not usually a vindictive sort but I recall hoping the driver

had something bad happen to them and then feeling guilty about that too. Poor creature. Strange how some memories are forgotten for so very long and then return with such clarity for no apparent reason.

The Forsaken

I mined my memories with no thought
for my own safety, no harness or shield,
as I capered down the corridors to catch
what cowered in the cognitive catacombs.

Something cringed in my consciousness,
as I stripped the valley, morose of mind,
forsaking the raw materials and abusing myself,
by removing the ore of opportunities

and culling the capacity to choose, to lose,
all that was left in the darkness, the harshness,
was a feral child, who would become oblivious
to pain and defiant, dead to me.

Exonerated Executioner

The gallows grow crowded
if we string up the fools,
better to let them fall
in love, that they may hang
and, if push comes
to shove, we can appease
our horror hungry hearts
by murdering the idiots,
those unable to grasp
the concept of lying,
fervid virginity,
the masquerade of dying.

Fade To Black

Shall I compare thee to a summer's day? Thou art more,
and the film starts showing images of verdant meadows,
and sunshine, and running, and laughter, all the pretty things.
The poem fades out and the music begins, the form lost
and the art swallowed by false imagery and imagined
romanticism, words whittled to a nub, such profound silence.

An Alternative Title Once Lived Here

I cried and no one noticed,
I screamed and not one person flinched,
I fell and absence caught me,
I would not wake when pinched,
I broke and bled, everyone fled,
I poured a glass of pity and spiked it,
Then I filled a page with unspent rage,
And every fucker liked it.

Sphere

I wish I had the lens
to capture such a sight,
a perfect moon broke
through the clouds
and bathed me
in its light,
a perfect circle stole my heart,
a secret of the night,
a nimbus, silvered scenes, unseen
before Pegasus's flight.

Piano

The piano plays a ballad,
slender fingers grace the keys,
the soft accompaniment
of the acoustic guitar,
strumming an orgasm
to the candles.
The magic of the music,
a shroud of atmosphere,
an old comfortable blanket,
a spectrum fades on a wine glass.
The rhythm of my breathing
is the river of my emotions,
erratic and dramatic,
a child lies beneath your heart
in the dream-time,
and I take a step over the edge,
into forever as tears streak
my painted mask.
The heart of mother is broken,
words are wordless,
the sign writer paints out the sky.

Only The River Knows

'Only the river knows
where it is going',
but it does not have a clue,
and if it did know
it would end up
in the sea,
incorporated
into a vast aquatic
non-existence,
losing its identity,
swallowed
by a cold ocean,
becoming insignificant;
it would change its mind,
halt its course,
turn back in panic
and flee to a flood elsewhere.

Feather

Tormented by the feather
that sits on my sill,
I would will worthy words
if it were a quill.
Oh, for ink, dark and rich,
like obsidian soup,
ripe for recounting,
thoughts to regroup,
to tell tales and write poems,
the full page, such a view.
Oh, to write, to have written,
such a dream to come true.

Librarian

Books, the great comfort,
a guilty pleasure (though
an obvious one) bookcases
bowing with the weight of
their glorious bounty, I could
happily scan the shelves
for hours, meticulously choosing,
my eyes are hungry, ravenous,
and greedy beyond belief for text,
the smell of parchment
seeps in to my soul, soothing me,
I open each volume at an angle,
squinting to read into the corners,
careful not to crack the spine,
bend a page or (oh horrors) tear a leaf,
dusty covers whisper to me seductively,
begging me to pick them, I want to
liberate the books from the library and
love them like my own, I cradle them
as children; revere each with such
wonder...I would write such a book
for others to love, to live for, yet
I ponder, if such a document is my
true desire, when I appear,
so petrified of the page...

Note from the poet: When other boys and girls were asked
what they wanted to be when they grew up, most responded
with announcements of 'fireman', 'doctor' or 'spaceman' (I
assume they meant astronaut as was always taught that if you
saw a spaceman, you parked in it, man). I said I wanted to be
taller and was laughed at, discounted before I realised I was a
thought or two ahead, thinking I would like to reach the top
shelves to discover what curious tomes slept beneath the dust

of our local (somewhat neglected) Eden (also referred to as the library). It didn't occur to me until I was nearly in double figures that I could be a writer! Yup! My childhood dream was to be a librarian because I thought I could buy a big house by reading all day. Thankfully, I have been blessed with well kept and well stocked libraries since and, although I don't borrow books anymore (my obsession now demands I purchase every book I desire when given the funds and opportunity so that it can forever reside in my own personal library) the library still caters for my needs, the majority of my first novel was written in libraries and, every now and then, I must go to one and wander the aisles dreamily.

Colour-blind

A world absent colour,
blight upon the eye,
love prefers a broader palette,
not shades that cry.
Friendship enjoys a tapestry,
of vibrancy and delight,
rid the world of races,
be one with all tonight.

Call Of The Wild

A whisper at the window
beckons me to the glass,
a susurrus, insensible,
until the moon has passed,
and wanderlust calls
another gypsy to roam,
long roads and endless halls,
so very far from home.

The Beloved Box

It lives in your shed, covered in dust,
protecting the letters of a lifetime,
the 'I miss you' notes,
the postcards, the thank you papers,
the 'darling' responses,
the 'dear beloved' poems;
your box of forgotten promises
and broken dreams.
The shards of shattered inspiration,
all those things you started
but never finished before
the next project came along,
or new lady in your life
distracted you
with whatever you needed
to justify the delay to yourself.
And time just scared the shit
out of you more than technology could,
because time left you behind faster,
and that was the thing, wasn't it?
being left behind.
It was always easier to leave first,
you could pass the blame
and leave abandonment off your list.

Curtains

Faded films about ghosts
echo down the halls
of places where I used to live.
Drawn curtains, closing-in-walls,
pictures that seem absent of colour,
torn up, discarded, no more;
even the silence is too much noise,
dreams just dirty the floor.

Scream without making a sound,
the reflection of someone lost,
a deaths-head grin, wearing thin,
dark stains, bitter frost,
life without flavour, distasteful behaviour,
a saviour left in the dust,
a tombstone, the only legacy,
of a life lived because I must.

Baldy And The Blogs

Kieran Davis writes under the pseudonym of 'Baldy', a name that many in the blogging game have come to associate with fun and friendliness. His fantasy site, The Chronicles of Cyralost, documents the intricacies of his mythological world and provides readers with both poetry and fiction. This world features in his novel, which can be found at https://baldmythology.wordpress.com

Kieran's popular poetry blog, Baldypoems, has been offered numerous awards, gained a healthy following, and provided poetry that has been shared on many sites. It is thanks to Polly Stretton that Baldypoems exists. Polly, a renowned poet and fellow member of the Worcester Writers' Circle, showed Kieran how to set up the site and has continued to support and encourage since. You can find Polly's blog at http://journalread.com

Baldypoems has been a wonderful platform for Kieran to share poems and poetry, and enabled him to meet bloggers of influence, to make fantastic friends, and be a part of a magnificent writing community. WordPress has a lot to be thanked for. You can find Baldypoems at https://kdavisfanclub.wordpress.com

Kieran has no hair. He is fine with this. He has no issue with bald jokes and invites original ones as he writes seriously but never takes himself so.

About The Poet

Kieran lives in Worcester with his beautiful wife and children, he is a chef and writes whenever possible. Published in more than thirty anthologies and magazines, Kieran has made many appearances in *Carillon* magazine.

A keen advocate for writers and the written word, Kieran supports local events when able. He is a proud member of the Worcester Writers' Circle, a diverse group of highly talented individuals, who have helped hone his craft.

Kieran is also a writer of fantasy fiction with short stories in publications such as *The Top-hat Raven* and *Orcs & Aliens* and he is currently editing his first novel.

His first love has always been poetry and his popular poetry blog, *Baldypoems*, reflects this. Kieran believes there is a big difference between writing a poem and writing poetry. He says, 'Anyone can write a poem, but only a poet can write poetry.'

Kieran is a self-professed nerd (claiming to have been a geek before it was cool to be one) and collects books, bookmarks and numerous other treasures that drive his wife nuts. He also claims to be the luckiest man alive, proof that luck and fortunes are not related (because he is skint).

Acknowledgements

Thank you, thank you, thank you! It has been a genuine pleasure to work with Black Pear Press. I would like to take this opportunity to thank my publisher for working with me on *Lacuna*. I am immensely proud of this book, largely because of the professional, dedicated team behind it. The Black Pear Press website is well worth a peek, and I highly recommend their other titles. Please visit: https://blackpear.net

In particular, a special recognition is due to Polly Stretton. Dear Polly, I cannot begin to thank you enough for your time, support and love. My poetry is better because of you.

Thank you to my beloved brother Damien Davis. Damo, your cover photo is amazing. *Lacuna* is a more remarkable book because of it. I urge people to visit my talented brother's photography website here: http://damiendavis.co.uk

Thank you to David Lloyd-Rumens at Sub Studio Photography for the profile picture, great job, shame about the fugly bloke you photo'd! For a wonderful family portrait and excellent experience, please visit David at: http://www.substudiophotography.com

Thank you to the team from the Worcestershire Literary Festival and Fringe, it has been an honour to perform in your events and a delight to be involved with some of Worcestershire's finest writers. Thank you to Martin Driscoll for your time and support. The LitFest web site can be found here: https://worcslitfest.co.uk

Thank you to my online pals, members of the WordPress community, Ryan Summers, Michelle Taylor, Charles Yallowitz (http://legendsofwindemere.com) for your continued promotions, T.J. Therien – for your kindness, Paul F. Lenzi (http://poesypluspolemics.com) for your wonderful book blurb, support, encouragement and friendship. I am blessed to know you all.

Thank you so much to the Worcester Writers' Circle, the most wonderful and diverse group of talented and caring individuals one could hope to meet. Joining this group was one of the best things I ever did. I am a better writer and happier person because of you.

Thank you, of course, to my loving family and friends, proud parents and proudest grandmother ever. There really are not the right words to portray how I feel about you.

And finally, most importantly, thank you to my wonderful wife and beautiful children. All that I am, all that I do, it is all for you.

Kieran Davis